W9-CCI-784

IN THEIR OWN WORDS

Dear Son,
Thank you for ...
I hope you are ...
... in Hawaii. T...
... Kansas. The w...
beautiful. You ...
send their love. ...
that you will be ...
and visit us? ...

PEARL HARBOR

A Primary Source History

Jacqueline Laks Gorman

Gareth Stevens
Publishing

KEY TO SYMBOLS
The following symbols highlight the sources of material from the past.

FILM EXCERPT *Primary source material from a film about the subject matter.*

SONG/POEM *Text from songs or poems about the subject matter.*

OFFICIAL SPEECH *Transcribed words from official government speeches.*

GOVERNMENT DOCUMENT *Text extracted from an official government document.*

LETTER *Text from a letter written by a participant in the events.*

PLAQUE/INSCRIPTION *Text taken from plaques or monuments erected in memory of events described in this book.*

INTERVIEW/BOOK EXTRACT *Text from an interview or a book.*

NEWSPAPER ARTICLE *Extracts from newspapers of the period.*

TELEGRAM *Text from a telegram sent to or by a participant in the events.*

Cover photos:
Top left: A Japanese fighter pilot who took part in the attack on Pearl Harbor on December 7, 1941.
Top right: A letter written by a father to his son, a U.S. sailor who was stationed at Pearl Harbor in 1941.
Background: A Japanese fighter pilot takes to the skies over Pearl Harbor in Hawaii.

CONTENTS

Above: A map shows the location of Pearl Harbor, on the Hawaiian island of Oahu in the Pacific Ocean.

December 7, 1941, was a sunny Sunday in Hawaii. Suddenly, early in the morning while many people slept, Japanese bombers launched a surprise attack on the U.S. naval base at Pearl Harbor. In less than two hours, the attacking planes destroyed hundreds of U.S. planes and ships. More than 3,500 Americans—including civilians—were killed or wounded. With this act, everything changed for the United States and the world.

World War II had been going on in Europe since 1939, with the Axis nations of Germany and Italy fighting Britain and other Allied nations. Before the attack, the United States was officially neutral in the war. It was at peace with all other countries, including Japan, which was part of the Axis powers. Americans were shocked and angered by the bombings. A country that had not declared war on them had launched an attack on U.S. territory.

Before the attack on Pearl Harbor, most Americans thought that the United States would stay out of World War II. The United States was suffering from the effects of the Great Depression. Millions of Americans were out of work. Many people thought that the United States should concentrate on its economy rather than enter the war. Now, with an attack on U.S. territory, war could not be avoided. The United States entered World War II the day after Pearl Harbor was attacked.

Left: On December 7, 1941, Japanese forces launched a surprise attack on the U.S. Pacific Fleet, which was based at Pearl Harbor in Hawaii.

A year earlier, the United States had moved its Pacific Fleet from California to Pearl Harbor, a natural, sheltered bay on the south side of Oahu. At the time, Hawaii was officially a U.S. territory, located about 2,400 miles (3,862 kilometers) from the West Coast. Ford Island, at the center of the harbor, was where the Pearl Harbor Naval Station was located. Ford Island also had an airbase, oil storage tanks, and various buildings. Hickam Field, a large airbase, was located on Oahu to the south of the harbor. Japan hoped that by attacking Pearl Harbor, it could destroy the U.S. Pacific Fleet. In doing so, Japan hoped to prevent the United States from blocking Japanese efforts to take and keep territory in the Pacific.

Above: *"Remember Pearl Harbor" became a rallying cry for Americans as they pulled together to win World War II.*

Before Japan attacked Pearl Harbor on December 7, no one in Hawaii knew that several Japanese ships and planes were positioned about 200 miles (322 km) from Oahu. Beginning at 6 A.M., two waves of planes—350 in all—took off from Japanese aircraft carriers. Soon, they were flying over Pearl Harbor, dropping torpedoes and bombs on U.S. battleships, destroyers, and airplanes. The attack took less than two hours, but its effects were devastating. In addition to the more than 3,500 Americans who were killed or injured, many U.S. planes and ships were either completely destroyed or badly damaged. The Japanese had taken them by surprise.

After the attack, Americans no longer saw the world in the same way. On the mainland, before news about the attack was reported, three professional football games were being broadcast. The games were interrupted by the announcement of the attack. For the United States, the time for games was over.

Above: *With American men overseas, American women joined the workforce. Some took jobs in factories. The image of "Rosie the Riveter" became a popular symbol of the female factory worker.*

PLANT A VICTORY GARDEN

OUR FOOD IS FIGHTING

A GARDEN WILL MAKE YOUR RATIONS GO FURTHER

Above: *Women on the home front were urged to grow more of their families' food by planting "victory gardens" during the war.*

Below: *Crowds of people gathered outside the White House in Washington, D.C., as news of the attack on Pearl Harbor spread across the nation.*

The day after the attack, 90 million Americans listened to President Franklin D. Roosevelt's speech to Congress. He described the attack, calling December 7 "a date which will live in infamy." Roosevelt ended his speech by asking Congress to declare war on Japan. Within days of the attack, the United States had also declared war on Germany and Italy.

The people of the United States banded together to defend their country and honor the thousands of innocent people who had died at Pearl Harbor. Americans could no longer ignore what was happening in Europe and the Pacific. The war had been brought to American soil. Japan had

hoped that after attacking Pearl Harbor, the United States would be unable to fight in the Pacific. Instead, the attack inspired Americans to fight even harder. Millions joined the armed forces. Before the attack, fewer than 1.7 million people were in the U.S. military. By 1945, more than 7 million Americans had enlisted.

Hundreds of thousands of Americans took jobs in factories. They produced ships, planes, and weapons needed to fight the war. That increase in industrial production brought many people back to work. The war effort provided jobs, helped stimulate the U.S. economy, and end the Great Depression.

At the same time, the attack had an unfortunate effect on Japanese Americans. Many Americans were gripped with angry feelings for the Japanese after the attack. People were afraid that Japanese Americans were loyal to the emperor of Japan, not to the president of the United States. Many Japanese Americans were also victims of violence, especially on the West Coast. In February 1942, President Roosevelt signed a measure ordering the relocation of Japanese Americans from the West Coast. Some 120,000 people were forced from their homes, farms, and businesses to go to ten relocation camps, where conditions were harsh.

They had to stay there until the camps were closed in 1944 and 1945. Despite the fear, no evidence was ever found of spying or sabotage by Japanese Americans.

The world might be very different if Pearl Harbor had not been attacked. One of the biggest changes brought about by Pearl Harbor was the transformation of the role of the United States in the world. The United States was the only country to emerge from World War II as a stronger nation. After the war, the United States became a global leader with a revitalized economy and the world's strongest military.

Above: *A poster for the film* Tora! Tora! Tora!, *released almost 30 years after the attack, told the story of Pearl Harbor from both the American and Japanese viewpoints.*

Above: *This poster advertised war bonds. It showed leaders of the Axis nations: Italy's Benito Mussolini (1883–1945), Germany's Adolf Hitler (1889–1945), and Japan's Hirohito (1901–1989).*

7

Above: *The Japanese felt threatened by the U.S. warships that sailed into what is now Tokyo Bay in 1853.*

Until the mid-1850s, Japan had little contact with other countries. Ships from other nations were not allowed to enter its ports. Japanese people could not leave the country or have contact with foreigners. In 1853, a U.S. Navy officer named Matthew C. Perry arrived in Japan. President Millard Fillmore had sent Commodore Perry to establish trade relations between Japan and the United States. Perry's arrival ended Japan's isolation. His visit put in motion events that would eventually result in the Japanese attack on Pearl Harbor.

"I have directed Commodore Perry to assure your imperial majesty that I entertain the kindest feelings toward your majesty's person and government, and that I have no other objective ... but to propose to your imperial majesty that the United States and Japan should live in friendship and have commercial intercourse with each other...."

U.S. President Millard Fillmore (1800–1874) to Emperor Meiji of Japan, 1853

EMPERORS AND SHOGUNS

In the 1800s, Japan was ruled by an emperor who the Japanese people believed was descended from gods. The real power, however, lay with the shogun. The shogun was a military leader who governed in the name of the emperor.

Perry sailed into what is now Tokyo Bay on July 8, 1853. He came with four armed warships and 560 men. The Japanese felt threatened by Perry's ships, which they thought looked like "giant dragons puffing smoke." Perry delivered a letter from President Fillmore asking Japan to trade with Western nations.

Right: *Japanese Emperor Meiji reigned from 1867 until 1912, a time during which Japan underwent dramatic political, social, and industrial changes.*

"The United States of America and the Empire of Japan, desiring to establish firm, lasting, and sincere friendship between the two nations, have resolved to fix, in a manner clear and positive, by means of a treaty or general convention of peace and amity, the rules which shall in the future be mutually observed in the intercourse of their respective countries.... There shall be a perfect, permanent, and universal peace, and a sincere and cordial amity between the United States and the Empire of Japan...."

Excerpt from the Kanagawa Treaty (1854), that established trade between the United States and Japan

The commodore then left Japan. When he returned in 1854, he and the ruling shogun signed a trade agreement between the United States and Japan.

Over time, Japan changed. The country was exposed to Western culture. In 1867, various groups banded together to overthrow the shogun. They wanted to make the emperor more powerful. Although the emperor was supposed to be Japan's supreme ruler, the Japanese military was in charge. Under the military's direction, Japan developed a modern army and new industries. Japan also developed a desire for increased territory and greater power.

To increase its power further, Japan fought with other countries, gaining territory with each new war. Japan swiftly defeated China in the Sino-Japanese War (1894–1895). That victory gave Japan control over a group of islands located to the east of China. Japan defeated Russia in the Russo-Japanese War (1904–1905), a victory that also increased Japan's territory. That victory brought attention from the West, since it showed that Japan could defeat a powerful Western country. Japan annexed Korea in 1910. A few years later, during World War I (1914–1918), Japan fought against Germany on the side of the Allies (France, Britain, Russia, Italy, and the United States). At the end of the war, Japan got control of land in China that had previously been under German rule.

> "It is our hope
> That all the world's oceans
> Be joined in peace,
> So why do the winds and waves
> Now rise up in angry rage?"
>
> *"Universal Brotherhood," a poem by Emperor Meiji (1852–1912) of Japan*

TIME LINE
1853-1887

JULY 8, 1853
Commodore Perry visits Japan.

MARCH 31, 1854
United States and Japan sign the Treaty of Kanagawa, an exclusive trade agreement.

DECEMBER 1867
Japanese shogunate is overthrown.

DECEMBER 1887
United States gets full rights to use Pearl Harbor to establish a refueling and repair station for U.S. ships in the Pacific.

Above: *A scene from the Sino-Japanese War is shown in a nineteenth-century Japanese woodblock print.*

"We are a weak people, we Hawaiians, and have no power unless we stand together. The United States is a land of liberty. The people there are the friends— the great friends of the weak. Let us show them that as they love their country and would suffer much before giving it up, so do we love our country, our Hawaii, and pray that they do not take it from us...."

Emma Nawahi, addressing a group of Hawaiians in 1897 to oppose U.S. efforts to annex Hawaii

THE UNITED STATES AND HAWAII

The United States was also expanding into an overseas empire. Hawaii, an island group in the Pacific Ocean, had been an independent nation that was ruled by a royal family. In 1876, the United States signed treaties with the Hawaiian rulers to increase trade between the countries. Hawaii has many natural resources, and Americans wanted access to them. In 1887, the United States got exclusive rights to use Pearl Harbor on the island of Oahu. The Hawaiians called Pearl Harbor *Wai Momi*, which means "waters of pearl," because the water contained many pearl-producing oysters. The harbor was a good place to repair and refuel U.S. ships that were traveling in the Pacific. To increase trade with Hawaii, the United States influenced Hawaii's transition from a royal monarchy to an independent republic in 1893. In 1898, U.S. President William McKinley signed the Newlands Resolution, a bill to annex Hawaii. The Hawaiian islands became U.S. territory in 1900.

Above: *The U.S. flag was raised at Iolani Palace in Honolulu during ceremonies to mark the U.S. annexation of Hawaii in 1898.*

A PACIFIC EMPIRE

The United States defeated Spain in the Spanish–American War (1898). As a result, the United States gained control of Guam and the Philippines, located near Japan, and Puerto Rico, located about 1,000 miles (1,609 km) off the coast of Florida. At the same time, the United States became active in China. Various nations had begun getting control of parts of China at the end of the 1800s. To increase trade, the United States developed the Open Door Policy. That was an informal agreement with Britain, France, Germany, Russia, Italy, and Japan, guaranteeing equal trading rights with China and those countries.

Right: *Queen Lili'uokalani (1838–1937) the last monarch to rule Hawaii, was overthrown in 1893.*

JAPANESE EXPANSION

Japan was not pleased by the growing U.S. presence in the Pacific. With its increasing population, Japan wanted to have its own Pacific empire. This desire became urgent after 1929, when the world was gripped by an economic depression. Japan needed more territory to get the resources and food it wanted and needed. Under Emperor Hirohito—who took the throne in 1926—Japan took steps to expand. In 1931, Japan seized the Chinese province of Manchuria. The United States supported China, but did little more than protest Japan's actions. In 1937, Japan invaded eastern China. News of Japanese crimes against the Chinese spread around the world. The United States protested again. It sent China aid and arms, but did little else to stop Japan.

"[Japan] is a most formidable military power. Her people have peculiar fighting capacity. They are very proud, very warlike, very sensitive, and are influenced by ... a great self-confidence, both ferocious and conceited, due to their victory over the mighty empire of Russia.... Moreover, Japan's population is increasing rapidly and demands an outlet; and the Japanese laborers, small farmers, and petty traders would, if permitted, flock by the hundred thousand into the United States, Canada, and Australia."

President Theodore Roosevelt, writing in 1909 to Senator Philander C. Knox, who was about to become Secretary of State under William Howard Taft

Right: *An injured child sits amid rubble after Japanese planes bombed Shanghai, China, in 1937.*

"The killing of civilians [in Nanking, China] was widespread. Foreigners who traveled widely through the city found civilians dead on every street. Some of the victims were aged men, women, and children.... Policemen and firemen were special objects of attack."

Journalist F. Tillman Durdin,
The New York Times, December 18, 1937,
during the Japanese invasion of China

TIME LINE 1893-1937

1893
Hawaiian queen overthrown; independent republic is established.

1894–1895
Sino-Japanese War is fought.

JULY 7, 1898
United States annexes Hawaii.

DECEMBER 10, 1898
United States acquires Philippines, Puerto Rico, and Guam from Spain.

SEPTEMBER 6, 1899
United States develops the Open Door Policy to increase east-west trade.

FEBRUARY 22, 1900
Hawaii becomes a U.S. territory.

1904–1905
Russo-Japanese War is fought.

1910
Japan annexes Korea.

DECEMBER 25, 1926
Hirohito becomes emperor of Japan.

OCTOBER 29, 1929
U.S. stock market collapses, beginning the Great Depression.

SEPTEMBER 18, 1931
Japan invades Manchuria.

NOVEMBER 8, 1932
U.S. President Franklin D. Roosevelt is elected.

JULY 7, 1937
Japan invades China.

Before the attack on Pearl Harbor, World War II (1939–1945) was a European conflict. The United States did not want to become involved in the war. It became difficult, however, for Americans to stand by while terrible things were happening throughout the world.

Above: Aviator Charles Lindbergh (1902–1974) believed that the United States should not become involved in World War II.

WORLD WAR II BEGINS

In the 1930s, Adolf Hitler became the dictator of Germany, beginning the events that would result in World War II. The war sent all of Europe into chaos, absorbing most of the world into a conflict unlike any other in human history.

Hitler had plans to expand Germany's territory throughout Europe. He began by annexing Austria in 1938 and Czechoslovakia in 1939. Since Britain and France wanted to avoid war, they let Hitler act without intervening. In August 1939, Germany and the Soviet Union signed a pact of nonaggression. It stated that the two countries would not attack each other. The pact cleared the way for Germany to expand its territory without Soviet intervention. Germany invaded Poland on September 1, 1939. This time, Britain and France were forced to act. On September 3, they declared war on Germany, starting World War II.

Germany easily defeated Poland. After several months with little fighting, Germany moved quickly in the spring of 1940 and invaded France, Belgium, the Netherlands, and other countries. By May, Germany had defeated all of them except France. However, France could not hold out for long, so the French government signed an armistice (peace agreement) with the Germans on June 22. After that, Britain was the only country left to fight the Axis powers.

Below: German troops march into France in 1940.

Right: Adolf Hitler (far right), the dictator of Nazi Germany, attacked Poland in 1939, beginning World War II.

"It is now two years since [World War II] began. From that day in September 1939, until the present moment, there has been an ... effort to force the United States into the conflict.... We are on the verge of a war for which we are still unprepared, and for which no one has offered a feasible plan for victory—a war which cannot be won without sending our soldiers across the ocean to force a landing on a hostile coast against armies stronger than our own. We are on the verge of war, but it is not yet too late to stay out. It is not too late to show that no amount of money, or propaganda, or patronage can force a free and independent people into war against its will. It is not yet too late to retrieve and to maintain the independent American destiny that our forefathers established in this new world."

Aviator and isolationist Charles Lindbergh, September 11, 1941

TIME LINE
1938-1939

MARCH 1938
Germany annexes Austria.

MARCH 1939
Germany annexes Czechoslovakia.

AUGUST 23, 1939
Germany and the Soviet Union sign a pact of nonaggression.

SEPTEMBER 1, 1939
Germany attacks Poland.

SEPTEMBER 3, 1939
France and Britain declare war on Germany, beginning World War II.

SEPTEMBER 5, 1939
United States declares neutrality in European war.

NOVEMBER 4, 1939
United States passes Neutrality Acts.

U.S. REACTION

In the mid-1930s, the U.S. Congress passed a series of laws called the Neutrality Acts to keep the United States out of foreign conflicts. As World War II went on, however, Americans became concerned. Most were against Germany's actions, but many were also isolationists. They believed that government officials should not make partnerships with other nations, and that the United States should avoid wars that did not involve its own territory and self-defense. Americans did not want the United States drawn into what they saw as a foreign war.

At that time, many Americans felt that their country had too many problems of its own. The United States was still suffering from the effects of the Great Depression, which caused widespread unemployment and homelessness. When Franklin D. Roosevelt became president in 1932, he passed reform programs that improved conditions. President Roosevelt's New Deal policies created jobs in construction, industry, and the arts which helped put people back to work. Millions of Americans were still unemployed, however.

Above: *The U.S. Pacific Fleet was moved to Hawaii's Pearl Harbor in 1940.*

Above: *Men sign up for the first peacetime military draft in U.S. history, which was passed by Congress in 1940.*

Roosevelt was an interventionist—a person who did not reject the idea of political or military involvement in the affairs of other countries when it was necessary. Roosevelt realized that the United States would likely become involved in the war at some point. Although the United States was officially neutral in the war, Roosevelt slowly began to take steps against Germany. The U.S. Congress passed a new Neutrality Act in November 1939. That act allowed all Allied countries to buy U.S. arms and other goods on a "cash and carry" basis. That meant that the countries had to pay cash for the goods and transport them in their own ships.

Late in 1940, Germany bombed Britain and made plans to invade. Roosevelt acted again, convincing Congress to strengthen the U.S. military. In September 1940, he agreed to lend Britain 50 old destroyers that it needed. The same month, Roosevelt convinced Congress to pass the first peacetime military draft in U.S. history. In 1941, Roosevelt got Congress to pass the Lend-Lease program. Under that program, the United States loaned Britain battleships, planes, and weapons. Roosevelt also did something that got the attention of the Japanese. In May 1940, he transferred the headquarters of the U.S. Navy's Pacific Fleet from California to Pearl Harbor in Hawaii. The Pacific Fleet was the only force capable of defeating Japan's

Right: *President Franklin D. Roosevelt (1882–1945) often used radio addresses to talk to the American people.*

"It is easy for you and for me to shrug our shoulders and to say that conflicts taking place thousands of miles from the continental United States do not seriously affect the Americas—and that all the United States has to do is to ignore them and go about its own business ... though we may desire detachment, we are forced to realize that every word that comes through the air, every ship that sails the sea, every battle that is fought, does affect the American future.... At this moment there is being prepared a proclamation of American neutrality.... And I trust that in the days to come our neutrality can be made a true neutrality,... but I cannot ask that every American remain neutral in thought as well.... Even a neutral cannot be asked to close his mind or his conscience.... I hope the United States will keep out of this war .... And I give you assurance and reassurance that every effort of your government will be directed toward that end."

Radio address by President Franklin D. Roosevelt, September 3, 1939

JAPAN JOINS THE AXIS

In September 1940, Japan joined the Axis nations of Germany and Italy. Under their agreement, Germany and Italy approved Japan's goal of creating a Pacific empire. Japan was now able to take French territory in the Pacific, such as Indochina (Cambodia, Vietnam and other countries), and continue its war against China. Many believed that Japan would soon move against the Philippines, further increasing its reach. In response, Roosevelt stopped the sale of certain U.S. goods to Japan, including important resources like oil, steel, and iron. Japan saw these actions—as well as the transfer of the U.S. Pacific Fleet to Hawaii—as threats. Japan decided to takeover territory in the Pacific to get the oil it needed. First, though, Japan had to defeat the U.S. Pacific Fleet at Pearl Harbor.

Above: *Emperor Hirohito of Japan (left, in carriage) supported the efforts of his country in joining Italy and Germany during World War II.*

powerful navy. Japan feared that the United States might use Pearl Harbor as a launching point for attacks on Japan.

TIME LINE 1940

MAY 1940
United States transfers headquarters of Navy's Pacific Fleet to Pearl Harbor.

SEPTEMBER 1940
United States breaks Japanese Purple Code; learns of Japan's intention to refuse U.S. demands to pull out of Indochina and China.

SEPTEMBER 2, 1940
United States makes destroyer deal with Britain.

SEPTEMBER 14, 1940
United States passes first peacetime military draft.

SEPTEMBER 27, 1940
Japan, Germany, and Italy sign pact; Japan joins Axis powers.

"We're in the Army now.
We're not behind a plow.
We'll never get rich while
    diggin' a ditch.
We're in the Army now.

We're in the Army now.
We're in the Army now.
We'll never get rich on the
    salary which we get in the
    Army now."

*"You're in the Army Now,"
an early U.S. draft-
related song, 1940*

Below: *German, Japanese, and Italian officials sign the Tripartite Pact. The agreement united Japan with the Axis nations.*

Above: To reach Pearl Harbor, the Japanese military had to travel east across the Pacific Ocean from Japan.

Although the United States was neutral in the war, Japan considered it a threat to its desire for expansion. Many Japanese, including Admiral Isoroku Yamamoto, the commander of the Japanese fleet, considered the United States an enemy. Yamamoto called U.S. ships stationed at Pearl Harbor "a dagger being pointed at our throat." Under Yamamoto's direction, Japan attacked Pearl Harbor, hoping to destroy the U.S. Pacific Fleet and American morale.

PREPARING TO ATTACK

In January 1941, Yamamoto developed a plan to attack Pearl Harbor. It involved secretly moving Japanese aircraft carriers to locations near Hawaii and then launching bomber planes from their platforms. To improve the strategy, Yamamoto turned to Minoru Genda, a fighter pilot and staff officer. The final strategy that Yamamoto and Genda developed had four key points. The attack would use all types of bombing. Its main target would be the planes on U.S. aircraft carriers. To be successful, Japanese ships would have to refuel at sea. The attack would work best if it occurred early in the morning, as a surprise.

A RISKY PLAN

Beginning in April 1941, the Japanese Navy placed a spy in Hawaii named Takeo Yoshikawa. Over a few months, Yoshikawa, who supposedly worked for Japanese diplomats in Hawaii, toured Oahu. He set up a telescope in a window of a teahouse on a mountain overlooking Pearl Harbor. He used the telescope to count the U.S. ships

"As a diplomat I could move about the islands freely. I often rented small planes at John Rodgers Airport in Honolulu and flew around observing U.S. installations. I never took notes or drew maps. I kept everything in my head.... I knew what [U.S.] ships were in, how heavily they were loaded, who their officers were, and what supplies were on board."

Takeo Yoshikawa (1914–1993), discussing his activities as a Japanese spy in Hawaii, 1941

Right: Admiral Isoroku Yamamoto (1884–1943), the commander of the Japanese fleet, planned the attack on Pearl Harbor.

Above: *Japanese pilots and naval crewmen trained for months before the attack on Pearl Harbor.*

TIME LINE
1941

JANUARY 1941
Japan begins to develop plan to attack Pearl Harbor.

MARCH 11, 1941
Lend-Lease Act is signed.

APRIL 1941
Japanese spy Takeo Yoshikawa begins working in Hawaii.

and planes located at the base. Many officials in the Japanese Imperial Navy were largely against Yamamoto and Genda's plan at first. Then Yamamoto threatened to resign if the plan was not adopted. His opponents softened, and the plan moved forward. Japanese aircraft carriers were sent to the island of Kyushu. It had a bay that was similar to Pearl Harbor, so the Japanese troops practiced there. In October 1941, Emperor Hirohito named General Hideki Tojo as Japan's new prime minister. Tojo wanted to protect the territory Japan had gained.

Tojo and Hirohito were both in favor of disabling the U.S. fleet. With their approval, Yamamoto set December 7 as the date for the surprise attack on Pearl Harbor.

Above: *Hideki Tojo (1884–1948), the Japanese prime minister, supported the attack on Pearl Harbor.*

OCTOBER 1941
Hideki Tojo becomes Japanese prime minister.

NOVEMBER 1941
Japan and United States begin negotiations.

NOVEMBER 1941
Admiral Yamamoto sets date of Pearl Harbor attack.

> "We trained fiercely, morning, noon, and night. We never had a day off, except when it rained. And we knew that we were about to start a war with America. We were shown drawings of [U.S.] ships on large cards and told to learn them. Two of them were the *Pennsylvania* and the *Oklahoma*."
>
> **Yuji Akamatsu, a Japanese fighter pilot, 1941**

Above: *The battleship USS Arizona sailed under New York City's Brooklyn Bridge when it was put into commission in 1916.*

FALSE DIPLOMACY

For the attack to be a surprise, Japan needed to convince the United States that there was no chance of war between the two countries. Japanese diplomats began negotiations with U.S. diplomats in Washington, D.C., with the apparent goal of preventing war. The Japanese pretended to consider U.S. demands that Japan pull out of both China and Indochina, a region in Southeast Asia.

NO TURNING BACK

On November 26, while negotiations were taking place, Admiral Yamamoto ordered the Japanese attack fleet to set sail. The fleet consisted of six aircraft carriers (carrying more than 400 planes), nine destroyers, three submarines, two battleships, three cruisers, and seven oil tankers. The fleet was under the command of Admiral Chuichi Nagumo, an experienced torpedo specialist. Minoru Genda was the fleet air operations officer. Over several days, the Japanese fleet crossed thousands of miles of sea until it reached about 200 miles (322 km) from Oahu. It went undetected by the United States.

Japan's main target was the aircraft carriers found at Pearl Harbor. On December 6, however, Takeo Yoshikawa (the Japanese spy) reported that the carriers were out at sea. Genda was disappointed, but intent on attack. He changed the main target to Battleship Row: the seven battleships moored along the southeast side of Ford Island. The large, powerful ships—the USS *Arizona, California, Maryland, Nevada, Oklahoma, Tennessee,* and *West Virginia*—represented most of the U.S. naval power in the region. (Two other battleships were undergoing repair work.)

"By Imperial Order, the Chief of the Naval General Staff orders Yamamoto Commander-in-Chief of the Combined Fleets as follows:

Expecting to go to war with the United States, Britain, and the Netherlands early in December for self-preservation and self-defense, the [Japanese] Empire has decided to complete war preparation."

Message sent by the Japanese Imperial Navy, November 5, 1941

Right: *Even as their government planned the attack on Pearl Harbor late in 1941, Japanese officials Kichisaburo Nomura (1877–1964) and Saburo Kurusu (1886–1954) carried on diplomatic negotiations with U.S. officials.*

Above: *Japanese planes prepare to take off from their aircraft carrier to bomb Pearl Harbor.*

TIME LINE
1941

NOVEMBER 26, 1941
Japanese attack fleet leaves Japan for Hawaii.

NOVEMBER 27, 1941
U.S. officials send "war warning" to all Pacific bases.

BREAKING THE CODE

The Japanese did not know that earlier, in 1940, U.S. military intelligence had succeeded in breaking the Japanese communications code—called Purple—which was used to send messages to diplomats. U.S. intelligence decoded secret Japanese messages. During negotiations, the United States had assumed that the Japanese were going to reject U.S. demands to pull out of China and Indochina. After U.S. intelligence broke Purple, however, they confirmed that assumption.

Above: *A Japanese naval officer gives instructions to fighter pilots before the attack begins.*

"Although we hope to achieve surprise, everyone should be prepared for terrific American resistance.... Japan has faced many worthy opponents in her glorious history—Mongols, Chinese, Russians—but in this operation we will meet the strongest and most resourceful opponent of all.... Therefore you must take into careful consideration the possibility that the attack may not be a surprise after all. You may have to fight your way in to the target."

Admiral Isoroku Yamamoto at a meeting of Japanese pilots, November 17, 1941

PEARL HARBOR

Above: *This shows part of the machine that was used by the United States to decode secret Japanese messages.*

The Americans realized that Japan was going to attack the United States and declare war. The question was where and when the attack would take place. Most U.S. leaders believed the likely target was the Philippines. The Philippines are located near Japan and would be valuable Japanese territory. Few people thought that Japan would strike Pearl Harbor, a region so far from its homeland.

On November 27, 1941, U.S. military leaders sent a warning to the heads of all U.S. Pacific bases. Those men included military leaders at Pearl Harbor: Admiral Husband E. Kimmel, Navy commander of the Pacific Fleet, and Lieutenant General Walter Short, the Army commander of ground forces. They were warned to watch out for possible sabotage of equipment and property. As a result, General Short ordered that the planes at Pearl Harbor be lined up and arranged wingtip to wingtip, so they could be watched.

THE LAST MESSAGE

On the night of December 6, the Japanese government sent its diplomats in Washington, D.C., a long, fourteen-part coded message. The United States got hold of the message and began decoding it. The message indicated that Japan would reject U.S. demands. When President Roosevelt was given the information that night, he turned to his adviser, Harry Hopkins, and said, "This means war."

"The [governments of the United States and Japan] have been carrying on during the past several months informal and exploratory conversations for the purpose of arriving at a settlement if possible of questions relating to the entire Pacific area based upon the principles of peace, law and order, and fair dealing among nations.... It is believed that in our discussions some progress has been made.... Recently the Japanese Ambassador has stated that the Japanese government is desirous of continuing the conversations directed toward a comprehensive and peaceful settlement of the Pacific area...."

Telegram from the Japanese ambassador to the United States to the Japanese government in Tokyo, November 14, 1941

Right: *Admiral Husband E. Kimmel (1882–1968) was Naval commander of the U.S. Pacific Fleet at Pearl Harbor at the time of the attack.*

Right: *A view of Pearl Harbor two months before it was bombed.*

DECEMBER 6, 1941
Japan sends a coded message to its diplomats in Washington, D.C.

A LATE WARNING

The last part of the message, which arrived early on December 7, told the Japanese diplomats to break off negotiations with the United States at 1:00 A.M. Washington, D.C., time—which meant that war would then be declared. After the message was decoded, it was given to Roosevelt and the commanders of the U.S. Army and Navy. The U.S. leaders knew that a Japanese attack could take place at any time, but they still did not know where. Warnings were again sent to all U.S. Pacific bases, including Pearl Harbor. There was a five-hour time difference between the East Coast and Hawaii, so when it was early in Washington, D.C., it was even earlier at Pearl Harbor. The warning to Kimmel and Short was sent to a telegraph office in Hawaii, where it arrived at 7:33 A.M. A young Japanese-American messenger got on his motorcycle to deliver the telegram to military headquarters. By the time he got there, it was too late. The attack had already taken place.

"Vessels moored in harbor are 9 battleships, 3 Class B cruisers, 3 sea-plane tenders, 17 destroyers; entering harbor are 4 class B cruisers, 3 destroyers. All aircraft carriers and heavy cruisers have departed harbor.... no indication of any change in U.S. Fleet or anything unusual ..."

Message from Admiral Isoroku Yamamoto to the Japanese attack fleet, December 6, 1941

"This dispatch is a war warning. Negotiations with Japan looking toward stabilization of conditions in the Pacific have ceased and an aggressive move by Japan is expected within the next few days. The number and equipment of Japanese troops and the organization of naval task forces indicates an amphibious expedition against either the Philippines, Thai or Kra Peninsula, or possibly Borneo. Execute an appropriate defensive deployment...."

Warning message sent by the chief of naval operations to Admiral Husband E. Kimmel, November 27, 1941

Above: *A map shows the location of the U.S. battleships at Pearl Harbor at the time of the attack.*

Below: *A Zero, the main type of fighter aircraft used by the Japanese during World War II, soars in the air.*

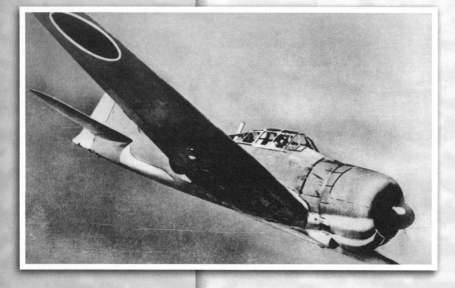

On December 7, Pearl Harbor was quiet. The Japanese knew that Sunday morning was the best time to stage an attack. Because U.S. sailors were caught by surprise, few were in position to fend off an assault. Many sailors were still asleep. The night before, the band from the battleship *Arizona* had won second place in a contest, so they were given permission to sleep late. The entire band—all between the ages of eighteen and twenty-one—died in the sudden attack.

THE ATTACK IS LAUNCHED

At about 5:30 A.M., the Japanese aircraft carriers were about 200 miles (322 km) north of Oahu, waiting for the signal to strike. The Japanese turned their radios to the Honolulu stations, which were broadcasting music. No one at the U.S. base Pearl Harbor suspected anything unusual.

At about 6 A.M., the first wave of the attack began. Under the leadership of Commander Mitsuo Fuchida, 183 Japanese warplanes took off from the aircraft carrier *Akagi*. The planes, which included forty bombers carrying torpedoes, took almost two hours to arrive. As each plane took off, the men on the *Akagi* cheered. A second wave of 170 planes left at 6:30 A.M. At 6:45 A.M., the U.S. destroyer *Ward* was on routine patrol near the entrance to Pearl Harbor. The crew noticed a strange movement in the water. There was a submarine there. The *Ward* fired on and sank the vessel, which turned out to be a Japanese "midget submarine"—a two-man sub carrying two torpedoes. Five midget subs had been released near the entrance to Pearl Harbor the night before. Lieutenant William Outerbridge, the *Ward*'s commander, radioed a report to naval headquarters, but officials did not take it seriously.

Above: *Five midget submarines like this one, each carrying two torpedoes, were released near the entrance to Pearl Harbor.*

Soon, there was another warning. At 7:03 A.M., two U.S. soldiers—Joseph Lockard and George Elliott—on duty at a radar installation on the north coast of Oahu, noticed strange blips on the radar screen. Those indicated a large group of planes was flying toward Oahu. They were only 130 miles (209 km) away. Lockard and Elliott telephoned the duty officer, Lieutenant Kermit Tyler. He incorrectly told them that the blips were a group of U.S. B-17 bombers on their way from California.

> "It was like the sky was filled with fireflies. It was a beautiful scene—183 aircraft in the dark sky. It was the most beautiful thing I had ever seen."
>
> **Japanese bomber pilot Abe Zenji, who was aboard the aircraft carrier *Akagi***

THE ASSAULT BEGINS

At 7:49 A.M., Commander Fuchida ordered his bombers to begin the assault by radioing, "*To! To! To!*" Suddenly, planes were roaring through the sky, dropping their bombs. Fuchida then radioed, "*Tora! Tora! Tora!*"—which meant that the Japanese had succeeded in surprising the enemy. Bombs struck the airfields at Kaneohe, Hickam, and other sites. Torpedo planes attacked battleships, destroyers, and cruisers. Within a few minutes, the battleships *California*, *West Virginia*, and *Oklahoma* were sinking. Many sailors were trapped belowdecks in the sinking ships; 429 men died on the *Oklahoma* alone. The *Utah* (an old battleship used for training) capsized with 58 men on board. Smaller ships were blown apart. The air was darkened by smoke, and the water was filled with thick oil that spilled from the sinking ships. The oil quickly caught fire, so the sea was covered with flames. Sailors jumped from the sinking ships. The most devastating blow was to the battleship *Arizona*. At 8:10 A.M., a bomb hit the deck of the ship, setting off ammunition on board. The *Arizona* exploded. Samuel Fuqua, the first lieutenant, bravely directed the crew to fight the fires and help the wounded before he was forced to flee. The mighty *Arizona* sank in nine minutes, killing its entire crew of 1,177 men.

6:00 A.M.
First wave of Japanese planes takes off.

6:30 A.M.
Second wave of Japanese planes takes off.

6:45 A.M.
Destroyer *Ward* sinks Japanese midget submarine.

7:03 A.M.
Radar shows large group of planes heading toward Oahu.

7:49 A.M.
Commander Fuchida signals attack to begin.

7:53 A.M.
Fuchida signals that attack was successful.

8.00 A.M.
U.S. radio message tells of the attack.

8:03 A.M.
Battleship *Nevada* torpedoed.

8:04 A.M.
Radio broadcast tells service personnel to report to duty.

8:05 A.M.
Battleship *California* torpedoed; battleship *Oklahoma* capsizes after being torpedoed.

8:10 A.M.
Bomb hits ammunition stockpile on battleship *Arizona*, which explodes.

By 8:35 A.M., the first wave of Japanese planes ended their attack. Twenty minutes later, the second wave arrived. They continued to hit the Kaneohe and Hickam airbases and pounded the remaining ships. Although the battleship *Nevada* was badly damaged, U.S. sailors tried moving it from the harbor so it could put up a better fight. The Japanese hit the *Nevada* repeatedly. It became clear that if the *Nevada* sank, it would block the harbor entrance. That would have created more difficulties for the Americans. To prevent their ship from sinking, sailors grounded the *Nevada* shortly after 9 A.M. A short time later, the last Japanese planes few back to their carriers. The attack was over.

Above: *Hit by a bomb, the battleship* Arizona *exploded and sank within nine minutes, killing 1,177 men.*

THE U.S. RESPONSE

Many Americans first thought the attack was a drill. Lieutenant Commander Logan Ramsey, on Ford Island, thought so too, until he saw a low-flying plane drop a bomb just before 8 A.M. He immediately sent out an urgent radio message to all ships and bases: "AIR RAID ON PEARL HARBOR. THIS IS NO DRILL." At 8:04 A.M., a Honolulu radio station interrupted its program to broadcast: "All Army, Navy, and Marine personnel to report to duty."

"Well, I was out on deck doing the morning chores.... All of a sudden, this plane came along, and [I] didn't pay much attention to it, because planes were landing at Ford Island all the time. And all of a sudden, the chips started flying all around me and the plane—it was strafing me.... I started back to my battle station and a bomb went off. I learned later it was back about turret number 4—about where I'd been working just minutes before. And evidently it knocked me out, ruptured both my lungs.... I don't know how long I laid there...."

Carl Carson, who was aboard the battleship Arizona *during the attack, 1941*

Above: *Rescuers approached the battleship* West Virginia, *which was burning and sinking after being bombed.*

"I saw a torpedo drop and our guns were firing before they'd even sounded general orders. I ran to my battle station and went through the rest of that day without getting fully dressed.... We could clearly see the *Arizona* and all of Battleship Row from our post. At one point we were all just standing there with tears in our eyes watching the devastation and feeling helpless, with nothing to be done about it."

Crewman Bill Speer, who was on the cruiser
Honolulu when the attack began, 1941

TIME LINE
Dec. 7, 1941

8:35 A.M.
First attack ends; Roosevelt speaks with U.S. secretary of state about the attack.

8:55 A.M.
Second attack begins; battleship *Nevada* gets under way.

9 A.M.
Crew of *Arizona* abandons ship.

9:10 A.M.
Nevada runs aground.

9:25 A.M.
Cruisers *Honolulu, St. Louis, San Francisco,* and *New Orleans* are bombed.

9:45 A.M.
Attack ends; Two-thousand four hundred and three Americans dead, including 68 civilians, and 1,178 servicemen and civilians wounded. Twenty-one ships of the U.S. Pacific Fleet are sunk or damaged. More than 180 aircraft are destroyed.

The Americans quickly realized that the attackers were Japanese. They could tell from the red circles—the symbol of the rising sun—painted on the planes' tails and wingtips. Some of the planes flew so low that Americans could see the pilots' faces. Sailors, soldiers, and airmen rushed to their battle stations. They manned guns and fought back as best they could. Since the U.S. planes were arranged wingtip to wingtip, they were not ready to fly. Fourteen pilots managed to get their planes in the air, however. They shot down at least twenty Japanese planes and several submarines.

Above: *Destroyer USS Shaw exploded during the early morning air attack by the Japanese on Pearl Harbor.*

"above and beyond the call of duty"

DORIE MILLER
Received the Navy Cross at Pearl Harbor, May 27, 1912

Above: *A poster shows Dorie Miller (1919–1944) wearing his Navy Cross medal (below).*

"It wasn't hard. I just pulled the trigger and she worked fine. I had watched the others with these guns. I guess I fired for about fifteen minutes. I think I got one of those Jap planes. They were diving pretty close to us."

Dorie Miller remembering how he used a machine gun on the West Virginia during the attack, 1941

"You understood exactly who they were, right away. I mean, you saw the Japanese rising sun on [the planes]. I just started immediately for my battle station.... They had a job to do, ... just like what we had to do, but the simple thing is that when you get in a ring with a boxer or a fighter, you know who you're going against. But when a sneak attack like that, it's something you have to think about, really think about."

Seaman First Class John Martini, who was aboard the battleship **Arizona,** *1941*

Doris (Dorie) Miller was one of the many brave sailors who responded. Miller, an African American, was a cook's assistant on the *West Virginia.* After the ship was torpedoed, he manned a machine gun even though he had never been trained to use it. Miller became the first African American to receive the Navy Cross, the second-highest award for combat heroism. Soldiers and sailors at Pearl Harbor received many awards for their bravery that day, including 15 Medals of Honor, 51 Navy Crosses, and 69 Silver Stars. Although Americans showed great heroism, they were also confused. Americans shot at twelve U.S. B-17s arriving from California and fourteen scout bombers from the aircraft carrier *Enterprise.* Some U.S. planes were shot down by friendly fire.

ASSESSING THE DAMAGE

At 11 A.M., Fuchida flew over Pearl Harbor to see the massive damage. It was the worst naval disaster in U.S. history. Twenty-one U.S. ships were sunk or damaged, including eight battleships; 180 planes were destroyed and 159 damaged. The Japanese lost only 29 planes and five midget submarines. The loss of life was huge: 2,335 U.S. sailors, soldiers, and airmen were killed, and 1,178 were hurt. Sixty-eight civilians were killed, and 35 were injured. The Japanese lost 64 men.

Right: *Admiral Chester W. Nimitz (1885–1966) awards Miller the Navy Cross for his heroism.*

Above: American servicemen salvaged what they could from the wreckage of U.S. warships damaged or sunk following the attack on Pearl Harbor.

RESCUE AND RECOVERY

After the attack, everyone joined in the rescue efforts. Sailors were trapped in some of the ships that had sunk. Rescuers drilled through steel walls to reach them. On December 9, two days after the attack, Americans rejoiced. Thirty-two crew members were found alive inside the *Oklahoma*.

Luckily, the repair facilities at Pearl Harbor were not badly damaged. Work began right away. Most of the sunken battleships were refloated and repaired. Some of the cruisers and destroyers were also fixed. During the salvage efforts, workers recovered and identified the bodies of the men who had died. When workers repaired the *West Virginia*, they found marks on the wall of one compartment. It showed that some men had survived for 17 days before they died on Christmas Eve.

THE UNITED STATES DECLARES WAR

On December 8, President Roosevelt delivered a speech to Congress. He called the attack on Pearl Harbor "a day that will live in infamy" and asked Congress to declare war on Japan. The Senate voted 82–0 in favor of war. In the House of Representatives, the vote was 388–1. Three days later, Germany and Italy declared war on the United States. The U.S. Congress responded with a resolution authorizing the president to declare war on them.

TIME LINE 1941–1944

DECEMBER 8, 1941
United States declares war on Japan; Japan invades Philippines.

DECEMBER 11, 1941
Germany and Italy declare war on United States; United States declares war on them.

FEBRUARY 1942
Roosevelt orders evacuation of Japanese Americas.

APRIL 18, 1942
United States bombs Tokyo.

JUNE 4–7, 1942
United States wins Battle of Midway.

FEBRUARY 1943
United States defeats Japan at Guadalcanal.

JUNE 6, 1944
D-Day invasion of France takes place.

"I saw about fifteen or twenty stretchers with injured men lying on them. They were lined up head-to-toe.... There were more bloody wounds—caused by shrapnel—than I had ever seen in my life....

We started operating. The air-raid sirens blew. And we heard the roar of planes over the fragile wooden hospital. We had nowhere to go. We had a patient in the middle of an operation. The big bombers, heading for Pearl Harbor, flew so low that the vibrations shook the instruments on the table....

Caring for the wounded and dying went on for days. Schools were made into temporary emergency rooms.
The cafeteria was used for the operating room and the kitchen was used for sterilizing instruments. There were shortages of bandages and medicines. We were not prepared for the many hundreds of casualties."

Second Lieutenant Madelyn Blonskey of the Army Nurse Corps, 1941

Above: *Japanese officials signed papers of surrender aboard the USS Missouri in Tokyo Bay on September 2, 1945.*

THE COURSE OF THE WAR

During the next months, Japan advanced in the Pacific, taking Guam, Wake Island, and other territories. On April 18, 1942, sixteen U.S. B-25 bombers staged a raid on Tokyo, Japan. The raid did little damage. In May, Japan also took the Philippines. Even so, things in the Pacific began to change. The turning point came in June when the Japanese suffered a major defeat at the Battle of Midway, near Hawaii. The Japanese were on the defensive. American forces defeated Japan at Guadalcanal in 1943, took Guam in 1944, and were victorious at Iwo Jima and Okinawa in 1945.

Meanwhile, in Europe, U.S. forces joined the British in fighting the Germans. On June 6, 1944, Allied troops landed on the French coast for the D-Day invasion. They eventually retook Paris, the Netherlands, and Belgium. By early 1945, it was clear that Germany would be defeated. Hitler killed himself on April 30, and Germany surrendered one week later.

A NEW WEAPON

Despite Germany's defeat, Japan kept fighting. Harry S. Truman, who had been appointed vice president after Roosevelt died on April 12 of massive bleeding in his brain, knew that many U.S. troops would die if the United States invaded Japan. Truman decided instead to use a new weapon, the atomic bomb, on

Right: *U.S. Marines raised the flag at Iwo Jima in 1945—an important victory for the Allies.*

"Yesterday, December 7, 1941—a date which will live in infamy—the United States of America was suddenly and deliberately attacked by naval and air forces of the Empire of Japan. The United States was at peace with that nation, and, at the solicitation of Japan, was still in conversation with its Government and its emperor looking toward the maintenance of peace in the Pacific....

The attack yesterday on the Hawaiian Islands has caused severe damage to American naval and military forces. I regret to tell you that very many American lives have been lost....

[A]lways will our whole nation remember the character of the onslaught against us. No matter how long it may take us to overcome this premeditated invasion, the American people in their righteous might will win through to absolute victory....

I ask that the Congress declare that since the unprovoked and dastardly attack by Japan on Sunday, December 7, a state of war has existed between the United States and the Japanese Empire."

President Franklin D. Roosevelt, congressional address, December 8, 1941

Above: An atomic cloud rises over Nagasaki, Japan. Japan surrendered after the United States dropped atomic bombs on two major Japanese cities in August 1945.

MARCH 16, 1945
U.S. victory at Iwo Jima.

APRIL 12, 1945
Roosevelt dies; Harry S. Truman becomes president.

APRIL 30, 1945
Adolf Hitler commits suicide.

MAY 7, 1945
Germany surrenders.

JUNE 22, 1945
United States captures Okinawa.

AUGUST 6, 1945
Atomic bomb dropped on Hiroshima.

AUGUST 8, 1945
U.S.S.R. declares war on Japan.

AUGUST 9, 1945
Atomic bomb dropped on Nagasaki.

AUGUST 14, 1945
Japan surrenders.

Japanese cities. Nicknamed "Little Boy," the first atomic bomb was dropped on Hiroshima on August 6, killing half the city's population of 300,000. (Another 100,000 Japanese died from radiation poisoning in the years that followed.)

JAPAN SURRENDERS

President Truman warned Japan that unless it surrendered unconditionally, more of its cities would face the same fate as Hiroshima. Three days later, U.S. bombers once again took to the skies above Japan. On August 9, a bomb nicknamed "Fat Man" was dropped on Nagasaki. It instantly killed more than 40,000 people. Five days after the second attack, Japan's emperor overruled the military, and Japan surrendered on August 14. World War II was finally over.

"We are in possession of the most destructive explosive ever devised by man ... We have just begun to to use this weapon against your homeland. If you still have any doubt, make inquiry as to what happened to Hiroshima when just one atomic bomb fell on that city."

Extract from the U.S. Air Force leaflet dropped on Japanese cities after August 6, 1945

Above: The Hiroshima Memorial honors the thousands of Japanese killed by the atomic bomb.

Above: *A propaganda poster from 1942 reminded Americans not to forget the attack on Pearl Harbor.*

Below: *During World War II, posters of Uncle Sam encouraged men to enlist in the military.*

I WANT YOU

for the U.S. ARMY ENLIST NOW

Pearl Harbor changed the way Americans saw the world. After the United States was attacked, Americans no longer believed that an ocean would protect them from harm. The attack also made them defend their country and honor those who had been killed. On December 9, 1941, The Oregonian—a newspaper in Portland, Oregon—introduced the phrase "Remember Pearl Harbor," something Americans have done since that tragic day.

NEWS AND SOCIETY

Americans knew that ships at Pearl Harbor had been destroyed, but they did not know the extent of the attack. They did not know that so many lives had been lost. In the days before television, many Americans got their news from newsreels, short films about current events shown in movie theaters. Cameraman Al Brick was in Pearl Harbor on December 7, 1941. He shot film of the attack. The U.S. government took the film from him. A censored version was released in February 1942. That newsreel and others about Pearl Harbor served as effective propaganda. They helped keep Americans in favor of the war and against the Japanese.

Outraged by the attack, Americans were united by strong feelings of patriotism. United States territory had never before been attacked by foreign forces. Although the United States was not directly attacked during the war, Americans were ready for battle. Teenage boys and men eagerly enlisted in the armed forces. Women and girls worked at home to support the war effort. With the men off fighting, many women went to work for the first time. Americans were united like never before.

"Down went the gunner, a bullet was his fate
Down went the gunner, then the gunner's mate
Up jumped the sky pilot, gave the boys a look
And manned the gun himself as he laid aside The Book, shouting
Praise the Lord and pass the ammunition!
Praise the Lord and pass the ammunition!
Praise the Lord and pass the ammunition and we'll all stay free!"

"Praise the Lord and Pass the Ammunition" by Frank Loesser, 1942

Above: *The phrase "Remember Pearl Harbor" became a rallying cry for the United States.*

DECEMBER 1941
Song "Remember Pearl Harbor" released.

FEBRUARY 1942
Censored newsreel released showing Pearl Harbor attack.

1951
Novel *From Here to Eternity* published.

1953
Film *From Here to Eternity* released.

1970
Film *Tora! Tora! Tora!* released.

2001
Film *Pearl Harbor* released.

"History in ev'ry century,
records an act that lives forevermore.
We'll recall, as in to line we fall
The thing that happened on Hawaii's shore.

Let's remember Pearl Harbor
As we go to meet the foe
Let's remember Pearl Harbor
As we did the Alamo.

We will always remember
How they died for liberty.
Let's remember Pearl Harbor
And go on to victory."

"Remember Pearl Harbor" by Don Reid and Sammy Kaye, 1941

PEARL HARBOR IN SONG

"Remember Pearl Harbor" became the title of a popular song only weeks after the attack. The lively march was written by Don Reid and the bandleader Sammy Kaye. It became one of the most popular songs of World War II. "Praise the Lord and Pass the Ammunition" was another popular song, written by the composer Frank Loesser. The song was based on the true story of a chaplain named Howell Forgy who was on the cruiser *New Orleans* during the attack. Forgy encouraged sailors on the ammunition line. His words to the sailors inspired the tribute song.

Above: *The cover of sheet music for "Remember Pearl Harbor" (1941), showed a streaked sky.*

Above: *Burt Lancaster starred in the 1953 film* From Here to Eternity, *one of many movies that used the story of Pearl Harbor as their plot.*

THE PRINTED PAGE

Thousands of nonfiction books and novels have been published about the attack on Pearl Harbor. One noteworthy historical book is *At Dawn We Slept: The Untold Story of Pearl Harbor* by Gordon W. Prange (1981). The book examines both the Japanese and American sides of the conflict. Many historical books trace the events leading up to the attack, while others detail eyewitness accounts of survivors. The fictional bestseller *From Here to Eternity* by James Jones (1951) tells soldiers' personal stories in the days leading up to the attack. More recently, Harry Turtledove's *Days of Infamy* (2004) looked at what might have happened if the Japanese had launched a full-scale invasion and occupation of Hawaii.

ON THE SCREEN

Movies have also used the dramatic story of Pearl Harbor as their plot. From the first film, *Remember Pearl Harbor* (1942) to *Pearl Harbor* (2001), each considered the attack from various angles. One of the most famous films about Pearl Harbor is the Academy Award winner *From Here to Eternity* (1953). *In Harm's Way* (1965) also focused on the personal lives of officers. *Tora! Tora! Tora!* (1970), made by American and Japanese filmmakers, traced the road to war from both countries' sides.

Right: *Ben Affleck played a daring pilot in the action film* Pearl Harbor, *which was released in 2001.*

The Final Countdown (1980) was a science fiction movie about Pearl Harbor. It asked: What would happen if a modern-day nuclear aircraft carrier was somehow sent back in time to December 6, 1941? Should the crew strike against the Japanese, or should they let history take its course? The filmmakers were helped by the U.S. Navy while making the film.

Above: *The movie* Tora! Tora! Tora! *(1970) retold the story of the attack from both sides.*

Some critics were disappointed by *Pearl Harbor* (2001), which starred Ben Affleck and Josh Hartnett as U.S. airmen. The film was released on Memorial Day and had dazzling special effects. However, it contained a few historical inaccuracies and drew criticism from survivors and historians. In spite of those criticisms, *Pearl Harbor* became one of the largest grossing films in history.

Below: *Pearl Harbor survivor and veteran Edmond Chappell signs an autograph during the 2001 premiere of Pearl Harbor.*

"On December 7, 1941, Japan like its infamous Axis partners struck first and declared war afterwards. Costly to our Navy was the loss of war vessels, airplanes, and equipment, but more costly to Japan was the effectiveness of its foul attack in immediately unifying America in its determination to fight and win the war thrust upon it and to win the peace that will follow."

The Bombing of Pearl Harbor, newsreel, 1942

Eightieth Congress of the United States of America
At the First Session

Begun and held at the City of Washington on Friday, the third
day of January, one thousand nine hundred and forty-seven

AN ACT

To promote the national security by providing for a Secretary of
Defense; for a National Military Establishment; for a Department
of the Army, a Department of the Navy, and a Department of the
Air Force; and for the coordination of the activities of the National
Military Establishment with other departments and agencies of the
Government concerned with the national security.

*Be it enacted by the Senate and House of Representatives of the
United States of America in Congress assembled,*

SHORT TITLE

That this Act may be cited as the "National Security Act of 1947".

TABLE OF CONTENTS

Sec. 2. Declaration of policy.

TITLE I—COORDINATION FOR NATIONAL SECURITY

Sec. 101. National Security Council.
Sec. 102. Central Intelligence Agency.
Sec. 103. National Security Resources Board.

TITLE II—THE NATIONAL MILITARY ESTABLISHMENT

Sec. 201. National Military Establishment.
Sec. 202. Secretary of Defense.
Sec. 203. Military Assistants to the Secretary.
Sec. 204. Civilian personnel.
Sec. 205. Department of the Army.
Sec. 206. Department of the Navy.
Sec. 207. Department of the Air Force.
Sec. 208. United States Air Force.
Sec. 209. Effective date of transfers.
Sec. 210. War Council.
Sec. 211. Joint Chiefs of Staff.
Sec. 212. Joint staff.
Sec. 213. Munitions Board.
Sec. 214. Research and Development Board.

TITLE III—MISCELLANEOUS

Sec. 301. Compensation of Secretaries.
Sec. 302. Under Secretaries and Assistant Secretaries.
Sec. 303. Advisory committees and personnel.
Sec. 304. Status of transferred civilian personnel
Sec. 305. Saving provisions.
Sec. 306. Transfer of funds.
Sec. 307. Authorization for appropriations.
Sec. 308. Definitions.
Sec. 309. Separability.
Sec. 310. Effective date.
Sec. 311. Succession to the Presidency.

Above: *President Harry S. Truman (1884–1972) signed the National Security Act on July 26, 1947.*

Days after the attack, an official investigation began into how the United States was caught off guard by Japan. That investigation was the first of many. Despite the tragic loss of life and the damage to the Pacific Fleet, the attack on Pearl Harbor did little to hinder the military strength of the United States.

WINNING THE WAR

Before 1941, the U.S. and Japanese military believed that battleships held the key to victory. World War II disproved that idea. Aircraft carriers turned out to be much more important than battleships in winning the war. At Pearl Harbor, eight U.S. battleships were damaged, and only six could be repaired. Fortunately, the Pacific Fleet's six aircraft carriers were not damaged in the attack. The U.S. Navy depended on them. As the war went on, the carriers were very important in winning major battles for the Allies in the Pacific.

Right: *A female war worker displays the freshly painted inside hatch of a submarine.*

"This is a victory of more than arms alone. This is a victory of liberty over tyranny. From our war plants rolled the tanks and planes which blasted their way to the heart of our enemies; from our shipyards sprang the ships which bridged all the oceans of the world for our weapons and supplies; from our farms came the food and fiber for our armies and navies and for our Allies in all the corners of the earth; from our mines and factories came the raw materials and the finished products which gave us the equipment to overcome our enemies. But in back of it all was the will and spirit and determination of a free people—who know what freedom is, and who know that it is worth whatever price they had to pay to preserve it....

As president of the United States, I proclaim September 2, 1945, to be V-J Day—the day of formal surrender by Japan.... It is a day which we Americans shall always remember as a day of retribution—as we remember that other day, the day of infamy."

President Harry S. Truman's radio broadcast after Japan surrendered in World War II, September 2, 1945

Above: *Women work in factories during World War II, producing arms and other war materials.*

TIME LINE
1942-1958

JANUARY 23, 1942
Roberts Commission releases report on Pearl Harbor.

1947
Central Intelligence Agency and Joint Chiefs of Staff created.

1950
Platform with flagpole built over sunken battleship *Arizona*.

MARCH 15, 1958
President Eisenhower authorizes creation of USS *Arizona* Memorial.

United States submarines were also very important in stopping the Japanese navy. The Japanese had not bombed the U.S. submarine base at Pearl Harbor, which was a big mistake. In addition, while the Japanese destroyed many American planes, they were older machines that were soon replaced by new, modern aircraft.

"They started somethin'
But we're gonna end it
Right in their own back yard!
We're proud of our country
And proud to defend it
So, Yankee Doodle, hit 'em hard!
Put our shoulders to the wheel
The whole darn world will get a brand new deal!
Oh! They started somethin'
But we're gonna end it
Right in their own back yard!"

"They Started Somethin' (But We're Gonna End It!)" by Robert Sour, Don McCrea, and Ernest Gold, 1941

"The Japanese attack was a complete surprise to the commanders and they failed to make suitable dispositions to meet such an attack. Each failed properly to evaluate the seriousness of the situation. Those errors of judgment were the effective causes for the success of the attack."

Excerpt from the Roberts Commission Report, January 23, 1942, blaming Admiral Kimmel and General Short for the attack on Pearl Harbor

Above: *Almost everyone did his or her part to help the United States win the war.*

Above: The USS *Arizona* Memorial at Pearl Harbor is a permanent reminder of the many lives lost when the battleship sank during the attack.

In fact, U.S. shipyards and factories produced new ships and planes very quickly to replace those that were destroyed at Pearl Harbor. The Japanese were unable to produce new weapons as rapidly.

The Japanese made another mistake at Pearl Harbor. They did not attack U.S. oil tanks and maintenance facilities. That kept U.S. oil supplies intact. The United States could repair and build ships and planes right at Pearl Harbor, which was closer to where the war was being fought. The Japanese also failed to attack an administration building at Pearl Harbor that contained a code-breaking intelligence unit. That unit provided information that helped the United States win the Battle of Midway against Japan in 1942.

OFFICIAL INVESTIGATIONS

Admiral Kimmel and General Short were relieved of their commands and had their ranks lowered shortly after Pearl Harbor. President Roosevelt appointed a commission to determine if the attack could have been prevented. The official commission, headed by Supreme Court Justice Owen Roberts, published its report in 1942. It said that Kimmel and Short were "solely responsible" for Japan's success. The report accused them of "dereliction of duty" for not making preparations to defend Pearl Harbor. Kimmel and Short retired in 1942. Kimmel said for the rest of his life that he was not given the information he needed to prepare for the attack.

Since then, ten additional investigations have examined the attack. Congress set up a committee that held hearings in 1945 and 1946, after World War II ended. As a result of those investigations, the Central Intelligence Agency (CIA) was created in 1947 to collect and analyze intelligence. The Joint Chiefs of

"The reasons for the disastrous defeat at Pearl Harbor form a tapestry woven of many threads, including the inevitable advantage of an aggressor free to choose the time, place, and form of a surprise attack in a time of nominal peace, and the brilliant planning and flawless execution by a Japanese Navy whose capabilities were seriously underestimated by many Americans.... The attack on Pearl Harbor probably could not have been prevented...."

Excerpt from the U.S. Department of Defense report on the attack on Pearl Harbor, 1995

Right: Members of Roosevelt's committee investigating the attacks on Pearl Harbor stood for photos.

Staff was created the same year to improve coordination and communication between the Army and Navy.

In 1995, the U.S. Department of Defense released another report. It stated that many people shared the blame for the United States not being prepared for the attack. The most serious mistake, according to the report, was Washington's delay in delivering the final warning to Hawaii on December 7. In May 1999, the Senate voted to recommend that Kimmel and Short be cleared of all charges against them.

Above: *This is the seal of the U.S. Central Intelligence Agency (CIA). The CIA was created by the National Security Act of July 26, 1947.*

TIME LINE 1961–2007

MARCH 25, 1961
Elvis Presley gives concert to raise funds for *Arizona* Memorial.

MAY 30, 1962
Arizona Memorial dedicated.

DECEMBER 15, 1995
Defense Department report says blame for Pearl Harbor should be shared.

MAY 1999
Senate recommends that Admiral Kimmel and General Short be cleared of charges.

DECEMBER 7, 2006
Groundbreaking held for *Oklahoma* Memorial.

DECEMBER 7, 2007
Oklahoma Memorial dedicated.

Above: *Fans cluster around Elvis Presley in Los Angeles, California, on his way to Hawaii to film* Blue Hawaii. *While there, Presley performed a the concert for Pearl Harbor.*

Above: The USS *Missouri* is now a memorial at Pearl Harbor.

After the terrorist attacks on the World Trade Center and the Pentagon on September 11, 2001, many Americans again remembered Pearl Harbor. In both 1941 and 2001, the United States had intelligence information, but did not act on it. "In Pearl Harbor there is not much doubt that the U.S. had received enough intelligence to predict the event, but failed to predict it," said historian Alan Brinkley of Columbia University. "Historians of intelligence argue that it doesn't matter how much information you have if you are not looking for what it tells you." U.S. officials in 1941 simply could not imagine that the Japanese would stage such a risky attack.

PEARL HARBOR TODAY

Pearl Harbor is now officially called Navy Region Hawaii. It is still an important military U.S. installation. It is the headquarters of five major fleet commands, including the Pacific Fleet. More than 80,000 people live and work there, including members of the U.S. armed forces, their families, and civilians. Pearl Harbor is also the site of the USS *Arizona* Memorial. The battleship *Arizona* was never raised from the sea, and the bodies of the 1,177 sailors who died there were never recovered.

Memorial Ceremony, USS Arizona, March 7, 1950

"We are here this morning to honor to the USS *Arizona* and her splendid crew, so many of whom are still with the ship. From today on the *Arizona* will again fly our country's flag just as proudly as she did on December 7, 1941. I am sure the *Arizona*'s crew will know and appreciate what we are doing."

**Admiral Arthur W. Radford,
commander in chief of the Pacific Fleet**

"May our efforts now be viewed as a solemn covenant to our fallen comrades, a covenant to complete the tasks which will help shape a better world for tomorrow. Grant that flag we are about to raise will ever stand as a symbol to our devotion to those virtues which have made our nation great."

**Captain E. B. Harp,
chaplain of the Pacific Fleet**

Right: *World War II veteran Paul Goody remembers the unidentified victims of Pearl Harbor.*

TO THE MEMORY OF THE GALLANT MEN
HERE ENTOMBED AND THEIR SHIPMATES
WHO GAVE THEIR LIVES IN ACTION
ON DECEMBER 7, 1941 ON THE U.S.S. ARIZONA

THIS MEMORIAL WALL WAS INSTALLED AND REDEDICATED BY AMVETS APRIL 4, 1984

Above: The names of the 1,177 men who died on the Arizona are engraved on this memorial.

"FROM TODAY ON THE USS ARIZONA WILL AGAIN FLY OUR COUNTRY'S FLAG JUST AS PROUDLY AS SHE DID ON THE MORNING OF DECEMBER 7, 1941. I AM SURE THE ARIZONA'S CREW WILL KNOW AND APPRECIATE WHAT WE ARE DOING."

ADMIRAL A. W. RADFORD, USN, MARCH 7, 1950
MAY GOD MAKE HIS FACE TO SHINE UPON THEM AND GRANT THEM PEACE

Plaque on the USS *Arizona* Memorial at Pearl Harbor

In 1950, the commander of the Pacific Fleet had a wooden platform with a flagpole built over the sunken ship. Many people thought there should be a permanent memorial to honor the dead on the USS *Arizona*. In 1958, President Dwight D. Eisenhower authorized the creation of the USS *Arizona* Memorial. The public fundraising campaign for the memorial began in 1958. In 1961, Elvis Presley performed at a benefit concert in Pearl Harbor to raise money. The fundraising was completed by 1961, and the memorial was dedicated on May 30, 1962—Memorial Day. Since then, 1.5 million people have visited the memorial each year.

MEMORIALS

The stark white memorial spans the middle section of the *Arizona*, which can still be seen in the water below. The memorial honors all the people who died during the attack. In December 2007, a new memorial was dedicated at a ceremony attended by Pearl Harbor survivors.

Below: The sunken wreck of the USS *Arizona* can still be seen below the memorial.

HOWELL FORGY (1908–1972)

Howell Maurice Forgy was born on January 18, 1908, in Philadelphia. After graduating from college, he worked as a miner before returning to school and becoming a Presbyterian minister. In October 1940, he joined the U.S. Navy as a chaplain and lieutenant. Forgy was on a cruiser during the attack on Pearl Harbor. He was preparing his Sunday sermon. Forgy encouraged the tired crew on the ammunition line by saying, "Praise the Lord and pass the ammunition, boys." His words became the lyrics of a popular song. Forgy served throughout the war, last becoming a commander. He retired in 1946 and became a civilian minister. He died in Glendora, California, in 1972.

MITSUO FUCHIDA (1902–1976)

Mitsuo Fuchida was born on December 3, 1902, in Nara Prefecture, Japan. While at the Japanese Naval Academy, he became friends with Minoru Genda. A skilled pilot, Fuchida flew air operations over China in the 1930s. He became a flight commander on the aircraft carrier *Akagi* in 1939. Fuchida was in command of the first wave of Japanese planes that attacked Pearl Harbor and was responsible for sending the radio signal "*To! To! To!*" to the other planes. After the attack, he became a national hero in Japan. He was wounded during the Battle of Midway in 1942. After the war, Fuchida converted to Christianity and became a missionary. He died near Osaka, Japan, in 1976.

SAMUEL FUQUA (1899–1987)

Samuel Glenn Fuqua was born on October 15, 1899, in Laddonia, Missouri. He served in the Army during World War I, then studied at the U.S. Naval Academy. In 1941, Fuqua was the damage control officer and first lieutenant aboard the USS *Arizona* at Pearl Harbor. When a bomb hit the *Arizona*'s ammunition stockpile, the ship's senior officers were killed, and Fuqua became the senior surviving officer. He directed the crew in fighting fires and rescuing the injured, in the middle of gunfire, fire, and heat. When he realized the *Arizona* could not be saved, he ordered the crew to abandon ship. He was among the last to leave. Fuqua was awarded the Medal of Honor in 1942. He retired in 1953 with the rank of rear admiral. He died in 1987 and was buried at Arlington National Cemetery.

MINORU GENDA (1904–1989)

Minoru Genda was born on August 16, 1904, in Hiroshima, Japan. He graduated from the Japanese Naval Academy and became a fighter pilot, flying missions in China. Genda was one of the first naval officers to recognize the importance of aircraft carriers. In World War II, he developed the plan to attack Pearl Harbor. He was also on one of the Japanese carriers during the attack. Later, Genda became a major general and chief of staff of the Japanese air force. Later, Genda said that if he had been in command in 1941, he would have repeatedly attacked Pearl Harbor and occupied Hawaii, using it as a base to attack the United States. He died in Tokyo in 1989.

EMPEROR HIROHITO (1901–1989)

Hirohito was born on April 29, 1901, in Tokyo, Japan. He became emperor when his father died in 1926. Hirohito ruled during a time when the Japanese military became increasingly powerful. Historians disagree about how much influence Hirohito had on Japan's actions during World War II. In early 1945, when Japan was losing the war, he refused to surrender, holding out until the United States dropped two atomic bombs. On August 15, 1945, the Japanese heard Hirohito's voice for the first time when his surrender speech was broadcast. Hirohito publicly rejected the view that the emperor was divine, gave up all but ceremonial duties, and cooperated with the United States during its occupation of Japan. He died in Tokyo in 1989 and was succeeded as emperor by his son, Akihito.

HUSBAND E. KIMMEL (1882–1968)

Husband E. Kimmel was born on February 26, 1882, in Henderson, Kentucky. He graduated from the U.S. Naval Academy, served during World War I, and commanded two destroyer divisions and a destroyer squadron. Promoted to admiral in February 1941, he became commander of the U.S. Fleet and the Pacific Fleet at Pearl Harbor. Shortly after the attack on Pearl Harbor, Kimmel was relieved of his command. He retired in 1942. Official investigations blamed Kimmel and General Walter Short of the Army for not preventing the attack on Pearl Harbor. Kimmel argued that he had not been given all the information he needed. He died in Groton, Connecticut, in 1968. His family continues to try to clear his name.

DORIS MILLER (1919–1943)

Doris "Dorie" Miller was born on October 12, 1919, in Waco, Texas. He joined the Navy in 1939. At Pearl Harbor, Miller was a mess attendant on the USS *West Virginia*, where he was also the ship's heavyweight boxing champion. He was collecting laundry when the attack began. Miller helped carry wounded sailors to safety, including the ship's captain, who later died. Even though he had not been trained to use a machine gun, Miller manned the gun until the order came to abandon ship. He was awarded the Navy Cross in May 1942, the first African American to receive the honor. On November 24, 1943, Miller was reported missing in action while serving aboard the USS *Liscome Bay*, which was torpedoed by the Japanese and sunk in the Pacific Ocean.

CHUICHI NAGUMO (1887–1944)

Chuichi Nagumo was born on March 25, 1887, in Yonezawa. Japan. He attended the Imperial Japanese Naval Academy and the Naval War College, becoming a specialist in torpedo and destroyer tactics. Promoted to vice admiral in 1941, he was appointed head of the Japanese navy's main aircraft carrier battle group and commanded the attack at Pearl Harbor. He won major victories in the Pacific but lost four carriers at the Battle of Midway in 1942—a turning point in the war. On July 6, 1944, during the Battle of Saipan, Nagumo committed suicide as U.S. troops approached. His body was found in a cave by U.S. Marines.

FRANKLIN D. ROOSEVELT (1882–1945)

Franklin Delano Roosevelt was born on January 30, 1882, in Hyde Park, New York. His distant cousin, Theodore Roosevelt, was also president of the United States. FDR, as he was known, was assistant secretary of the Navy and later governor of New York before being elected president in 1932. His New Deal programs helped revive the economy and restore hope to people who were suffering during the Great Depression. When World War II began, Roosevelt had the U.S. neutrality laws changed so that the United States could help the Allies. After Pearl Harbor, he directed the U.S. war effort and met with other world leaders to plan the postwar world. He was the only person elected to four terms as U.S. president. Roosevelt died in Warm Springs, Georgia, on April 12, 1945, with the end of the war in sight.

WALTER SHORT (1880–1949)

Walter Short was born on March 30, 1880, in Fillmore, Illinois. He served in World War I and had a number of important assignments before being promoted to lieutenant general and commander of the U.S. Army's ground forces in Hawaii in 1941. Short believed that his major role at Pearl Harbor was training. Both he and his Navy counterpart, Admiral Husband E. Kimmel, were blamed for not preventing the attack on Pearl Harbor. Both said they were innocent. Shortly after the attack, Short was relieved of his command. He retired from the Army in 1942 and went to work for the Ford Motor Company. He died in Dallas, Texas, in 1949.

HIDEKI TOJO (1884–1948)

Hideki Tojo was born on December 30, 1884, in the Kojimachi district of Japan. He studied at the Imperial Japanese Army Academy and the Army Staff College. He held many important armed forces jobs, before becoming a general and war minister, and commanded the Japanese army in China in the 1930s. In October 1941, he became prime minister, ordering the attack on Pearl Harbor. He was also minister of war, education, and commerce and industry. Tojo resigned in July 1944 when the war was going badly for Japan. After Japan surrendered in 1945, he attempted suicide. He was put on trial as a war criminal, found guilty and executed in Tokyo in 1948.

ISOROKU YAMAMOTO (1884–1943)

Isoroku Yamamoto was born on April 4, 1884, in Nagaoka, Japan. He served during the Russo-Japanese War and graduated from the Imperial Japanese Naval Academy and the Naval Staff College. Yamamoto was also posted for a time to the United States. He opposed Japanese actions in Manchuria and China and disagreed with Japan's alliance with Germany and Italy in World War II. Promoted to admiral and commander of the Combined Fleet of the Japanese Navy, he accepted the reality of the war and designed a plan to destroy the U.S. Pacific Fleet at Pearl Harbor. After the attack, he planned Japanese actions in the Pacific. Yamamoto died on April 18, 1943, in the Solomon Islands when his plane was shot down by the U.S. Army.

aircraft carriers Large ships with long, flat decks where planes can take off and land.

Allied nations In World War II, the nations that joined forces against the Axis powers; the Allies included Britain, the United States, France, and in the latter stages of the war, the Soviet Union.

ammunition Explosives that are fired from weapons, such as bullets and missiles.

annexed Took control of a country or region and made it officially part of another nation.

armistice An agreement to stop fighting.

atomic bomb A strong and destructive bomb that is powered by the splitting of atoms, tiny pieces of matter making up everything in the physical world.

Axis nations In World War II, the nations opposed to the Allied powers; the Axis was led by Germany, Italy, and Japan.

Battle of Midway A World War II battle fought in June 1942 between the United States and Japan near the Midway Islands in the Pacific; the battle was a major U.S. victory.

cash and carry A U.S. policy, passed in 1939, under which the United States sold arms and other goods to nations that paid for them in cash and carried them away in their own ships.

censored The planned removal of parts of a book, film, or play so the public does not read, see, or hear them.

chaplain A religious leader in the military.

civilian A person who is not a member of the armed forces.

cruiser A small, fast warship that is not as heavily armed as a battleship.

D–Day June 6, 1944, the first day of the Allied invasion of Europe during World War II.

destroyers Small, fast warships that protect ships from submarines using guns, missiles, and torpedoes.

dictator A leader who has complete power within a country.

diplomats People who represent their nation in another country.

draft A government system that requires people to serve in the armed forces if they are called upon.

emperor The ruler of an empire; in Japan, the emperor was believed to be all powerful and descended from the gods.

empire A group of nations, territories, or people ruled by a single country.

fleet A group of ships under a single command.

friendly fire The unintended strike of soldiers within troops from the same military unity.

Great Depression A period in the 1930s of massive economic decline, resulting in widespread poverty and unemployment.

intelligence Information about enemies or enemy actions.

interventionist A person who gets involved or interferes in something; in World War II, interventionists believed that the United States should help defend nations attacked by the Axis.

isolationists People who believe that their country should not get involved in the affairs of other nations.

Joint Chiefs of Staff The top military group in the United States that advises the president.

Lend-Lease Program A program, beginning in March 1941, under which the United States supplied weapons and other military goods to Allied nations.

naval base A military installation used by naval forces.

negotiation A discussion aimed at reaching a mutual agreement.

neutral Not taking either side in a conflict.

Neutrality Acts Several similar laws passed in the United States during the 1930s aimed at keeping the United States out of the affairs of other countries.

newsreels Short films about recent news events.

Open Door Policy The principle of equal trading rights for all countries in China at the end of the nineteenth century.

Pacific Fleet The U.S. Navy's naval force in and around the Pacific Ocean.

propaganda Information that is spread to influence people for or against a particular policy or idea.

Purple Code The secret Japanese communications code that was used to send messages to diplomats; the United States broke the code in 1940.

radar A system using radio waves to detect and locate objects.

relocation camps Temporary living quarters where people are held, especially during wartime.

Russo-Japanese War A war fought between Russia and Japan from 1904 to 1905, resulting in a Japanese victory.

sabotage The deliberate destruction or damaging of something belonging to an enemy.

salvage To recover what can be saved from a shipwreck or other disaster.

shogun The military governor who ruled Japan until 1867.

Sino-Japanese War A war fought between China and Japan from 1894 to 1895, resulting in a Japanese victory.

Spanish-American War A war between Spain and the United States in 1898, resulting in a U.S. victory.

surrendered When something is given up, especially when it is forced.

torpedoes Missiles that are launched through water to explode against a ship's frame.

treaties Formal agreements made by two or more groups or nations after negotiations, often at the end of periods of conflict.

U.S. territory A geographical area that belongs to and is governed by the United States but is not included in any of its states.

World War I A war fought between 1914 and 1918, mainly in Europe, in which Britain, France, the United States, Japan, and other nations defeated Germany, Austria-Hungary, and other countries.

World War II A war fought between 1939 and 1945 in which the Allied powers (Britain, France, the United States, the Soviet Union, and other nations) defeated the Axis powers (Germany, Italy, and Japan).

ACKNOWLEDGMENTS

Please visit our web site at: **www.garethstevens.com**.
For a free color catalog describing Gareth Stevens Publishing's
list of high-quality books, call 1-800-542-2595 (USA)
or 1-877-387-3178 (Canada).
Gareth Stevens Publishing's fax: 1-877-542-2596

A copy of the Cataloging-in-Publication Data is available upon
request from the publisher.

ISBN-10: 1-4339-0047-5   (lib. bdg.)
ISBN-13: 978-1-4339-0047-1   (lib. bdg.)

This North American edition first published in 2009 by
Gareth Stevens Publishing
A Weekly Reader® Company
1 Reader's Digest Road
Pleasantville, NY 10570-7000 USA

This U.S. edition copyright © 2009 by Gareth Stevens, Inc. Original
edition copyright © 2008 ticktock Entertainment Ltd. First published in
Great Britain in 2007 by ticktock Media Ltd., Unit 2, Orchard Business
Centre, North Farm Road, Tunbridge Wells, Kent, TN2 3XF, U.K.

Gareth Stevens Executive Managing Editor: Lisa M. Herrington
Gareth Stevens Editor: Joann Jovinelly
Gareth Stevens Creative Director: Lisa Donovan
Gareth Stevens Designers: Giovanni Cipolla, Ken Crossland
Gareth Stevens Production Manager: Paul Bodley, Jr.
Gareth Stevens Publisher: Keith Garton

Photo credits: B=bottom; C=center; L=left; R=right; T=top
20th Century Fox/Everett/Rex Features: 7T, 33T; AP/AP/PA Photos:
36-37; Courtesy of Michael Barnes: 31B; Bettmann/Corbis: OFC B
main, 5B, 11R, 12T, 15B, 18T, 18-19, 19CR, 20-21, 24T, 24B, 26L,
28T. 33B. 37BR. 40TL, 40TR, 41TL, 41TR, 41B, 43TR; British

Museum, London, UK/Bridgeman Art Library: 8T; Central Intelligenc
Agency: 37T; Check Six/Getty Images: 2; Corbis: 7B, 10BL, 11C,
16-17, 19T, 30B, 35B, 42TL, 42TR, 43TL, 43B; CSU Archives/Evere
Collection/Rex Features: 15T, 17CR, 31T, 42B; David J. & Janice L.
Frent Collection/Corbis: 5T; Everett Collection/Rex Features: 32T,
32B; Getty Images: 17T, 38B; Hulton Archive/Getty Images: 26T;
Hulton-Deutsch Collection/Corbis: OFC TL; Douglas Kirkland/Corbi
OFC T, background: Minnesota Historical Society/Corbis: 14T; Vito
Palmisano/Getty Images: 28-29; NARA: 21R, 29T, 34T; National
Security Agency: 20T; Naval Historical Center: 40B; Douglas Peebles/
Stock Connection/Rex Features: 1, 39B; Photo Resource Hawaii/
Alamy: 10-11; The Print Collector/Alamy: 8BR; Private Collection/
Archives Charmet/Bridgeman Art Library: 9B. Rex Features: 12-13;
Martin Sanders: 16T Shutterstock: 29B, 36T, 38T, 39T, 48; Sipa Press/
Rex Features: 4B; Tavin/Everett/Rex Features: 14B; Hayley Terry: 22
Underwood & Underwood/Corbis: 13BR; Witold Skrypczak/Alamy:
23T; Swim Ink 2, LLC/Corbis: 6T. Ticktock Media: 4T; Time & Life
Pictures/Getty Images: 6B, 25B, 27T, 34BR; United States Office of
War Information 30T; Roger-Viollet/Rex Features: 12B, 22B, 35T.

Every effort has been made to trace the copyright holders. We apologiz
in advance for any unintentional ommisions. We would be pleased to
insert the appropriate acknowledgments in any subsequent edition of th
publication.

Printed in the United States of America

1 2 3 4 5 6 7 8 9 10 10 09 08